Let's Discover Canada

NORTHWEST TERRITORIES

by
Suzanne LeVert

George Sheppard
McMaster University
General Editor

CHELSEA HOUSE PUBLISHERS
New York   Philadelphia

Cover: Inuit children in the Northwest Territories
Opposite: An Inuit musician with a skin drum

Chelsea House Publishers
EDITOR-IN-CHIEF: Remmel Nunn
MANAGING EDITOR: Karyn Gullen Browne
COPY EDITOR: Mark Rifkin
PICTURE EDITOR: Adrian G. Allen
ART DIRECTOR: Maria Epes
ASSISTANT ART DIRECTOR: Noreen Romano
MANUFACTURING DIRECTOR: Gerald Levine
SYSTEMS MANAGER: Lindsey Ottman
PRODUCTION MANAGER: Joseph Romano
PRODUCTION COORDINATOR: Marie Claire Cebrián

Let's Discover Canada
SENIOR EDITOR: Rebecca Stefoff

Staff for NORTHWEST TERRITORIES
COPY EDITOR: Benson D. Simmonds
EDITORIAL ASSISTANT: Ian Wilker
PICTURE RESEARCHER: Sandy Jones
DESIGNER: Diana Blume

First Printing

1   3   5   7   9   8   6   4   2

Library of Congress Cataloging-in-Publication Data
LeVert, Suzanne.
   Let's discover Canada. Northwest territories/by Suzanne LeVert;
George Sheppard, general editor.
     p. cm.
   Includes bibliographical references and index.
   Summary: Discusses the geography, history, and culture of
Canada's Northwest Territories.
   ISBN 0-7910-1031-7
   1. Northwest Territories—Juvenile literature. [1. Northwest
Territories.] I. Sheppard, George C. B. II. Title.
F1060.35.L48 1992
971.9'2—dc20

91-23011
CIP
AC

Contents

My Canada

by Pierre Berton

"Nobody knows my country," a great Canadian journalist, Bruce Hutchison, wrote almost half a century ago. It is still true. Most Americans, I think, see Canada as a pleasant vacationland and not much more. And yet we are the United States's greatest single commercial customer, and the United States is our largest customer.

Lacking a major movie industry, we have made no widescreen epics to chronicle our triumphs and our tragedies. But then there has been little blood in our colonial past—no revolutions, no civil war, not even a wild west. Yet our history is crammed with remarkable men and women. I am thinking of Joshua Slocum, the first man to sail alone around the world, and Robert Henderson, the prospector who helped start the Klondike gold rush. I am thinking of some of our famous artists and writers—comedian Dan Aykroyd, novelists Margaret Atwood and Robertson Davies, such popular performers as Michael J. Fox, Anne Murray, Gordon Lightfoot, and k.d. lang, and hockey greats from Maurice Richard to Gordie Howe to Wayne Gretzky.

The real shape of Canada explains why our greatest epic has been the building of the Pacific Railway to unite the nation from

sea to sea in 1885. On the map, the country looks square. But because the overwhelming majority of Canadians live within 100 miles (160 kilometers) of the U.S. border, in practical terms the nation is long and skinny. We are in fact an archipelago of population islands separated by implacable barriers—the angry ocean, three mountain walls, and the Canadian Shield, that vast desert of billion-year-old rock that sprawls over half the country, rich in mineral treasures, impossible for agriculture.

Canada's geography makes the country difficult to govern and explains our obsession with transportation and communication. The government has to be as involved in railways, airlines, and broadcasting networks as it is with social services such as universal medical care. Rugged individualism is not a Canadian quality. Given the environment, people long ago learned to work together for security.

It is ironic that the very bulwarks that separate us—the chiseled peaks of the Selkirk Mountains, the gnarled scarps north of Lake Superior, the ice-choked waters of the Northumberland Strait —should also be among our greatest attractions for tourists and artists. But if that is the paradox of Canada, it is also the glory.

Auyuittuq National Park is a pristine wilderness of glacial valleys and ice-capped peaks on the west coast of Baffin Island, just north of the Arctic Circle. The rock pile is a cairn made by the island's Native American inhabitants to mark a trail.

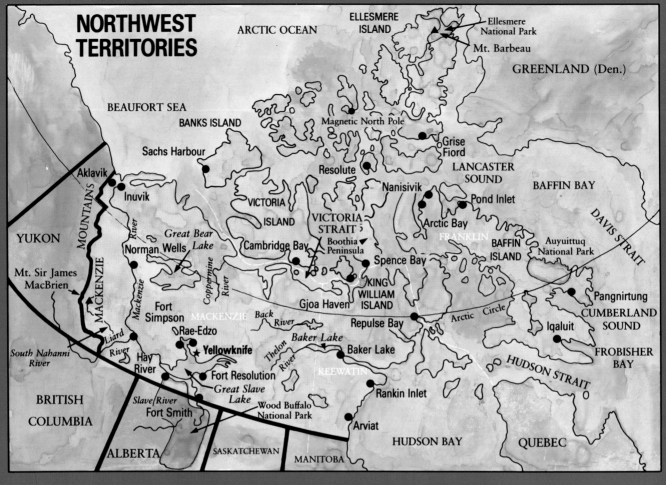

NORTHWEST TERRITORIES

ARCTIC OCEAN

ELLESMERE ISLAND

Ellesmere National Park

Mt. Barbeau

GREENLAND (Den.)

BEAUFORT SEA

BANKS ISLAND

Magnetic North Pole

Grise Fiord

Sachs Harbour

Resolute

LANCASTER SOUND

BAFFIN BAY

Aklavik

Inuvik

YUKON

MOUNTAINS

MACKENZIE

River

VICTORIA ISLAND

Nanisivik

Pond Inlet

Arctic Bay

VICTORIA STRAIT

FRANKLIN

BAFFIN ISLAND

DAVIS STRAIT

Great Bear Lake

Norman Wells

Cambridge Bay

Boothia Peninsula

Auyuittuq National Park

Mt. Sir James MacBrien

Mackenzie

Coppermine River

Spence Bay

Pangnirtung

CUMBERLAND SOUND

Fort Simpson

MACKENZIE

KING WILLIAM ISLAND

Liard

Back River

Gjoa Haven

Arctic Circle

Iqaluit

Rae-Edzo

River

★ Yellowknife

Repulse Bay

FROBISHER BAY

South Nahanni River

Hay River

Thelon River

Baker Lake

KEEWATIN

Baker Lake

HUDSON STRAIT

Fort Resolution

Great Slave Lake

BRITISH COLUMBIA

Slave River

Fort Smith

Wood Buffalo National Park

Rankin Inlet

ALBERTA

SASKATCHEWAN

MANITOBA

Arviat

HUDSON BAY

QUEBEC

CANADA

UNITED STATES

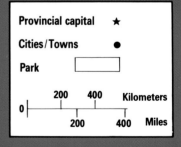

Provincial capital	★
Cities / Towns	●
Park	▭

200   400   Kilometers

0

200   400   Miles

Mountain aven

Gyrfalcon

Northwest Territories at a Glance

Population: 52,238 (1986 census)—11th among Canada's provinces and territories
Area: 1,304,903 square miles (3,376,689 square kilometers)—largest of Canada's provinces and territories
Highest point: Mt. Sir James MacBrien, 9,062 feet (2,746 meters)
Major rivers: Mackenzie, Coppermine, Thelon, Back, Anderson
Major lakes: Great Bear, Great Slave
Capital: Yellowknife (population 11,753)
Other communities: Inuvik (population 3,389), Hay River (population 2,964), Iqaluit (population 2,947)
Entered Dominion of Canada: 1870

Principal products: Gold, lead, zinc, silver, radioactive minerals, oil and natural gas, timber, fish
Government: The Northwest Territories is divided into three administrative districts—Keewatin, Mackenzie, and Franklin; the formal head of government is a commissioner, appointed by the federal government; the 24-member legislative assembly chooses a government leader, who is the executive officer of the territorial administration; the territories is represented by a senator and two members of the House of Commons in the federal government in Ottawa

The Land

With an area of 1,304,903 square miles (3,376,689 square kilometers), the Northwest Territories is the largest of Canada's provinces and territories; it covers a third of the country and is about the size of India, or more than one-third the size of the United States. With rugged mountains, broad river valleys, pine forests, vast tracts of frozen tundra, and ice-capped Arctic islands, the Northwest Territories is one of the last true wildernesses in North America.

The NWT, as the Territories is generally called, is located in northern Canada. On its east, across Baffin Bay, is the island of Greenland, which is owned by Denmark. On its southeast, across Hudson Bay, is the province of Quebec. On its south are the provinces of Manitoba, Saskatchewan, Alberta, and British Columbia. On its west is the Yukon Territory. In the north, the Northwest Territories extends to within 500 miles (800 kilometers) of the North Geographic Pole; the North Magnetic Pole, which is different from the Geographic Pole and moves about the Arctic Regions from time to time, is presently located within the

Opposite: The Mackenzie, Canada's longest river, flows north from Great Slave Lake and empties into the ice-choked Beaufort Sea. Over the centuries, the river has been a highway for migration, exploration, and trade in the far north.
Above: Young foxes bask in the sun amid wildflowers during the brief Arctic summer.

NWT about 200 miles (320 kilometers) north of the town of Resolute. The Northwest Territories includes the Arctic islands north of the Canadian mainland and all of the islands in Hudson, James, and Ungava bays. More than half of the NWT is located north of the Arctic Circle.

Three-quarters of the NWT lies on a vast bedrock formation called the Canadian Shield, which covers much of northern North America and contains some of the oldest known surface rock in the world—dating back about 570 million years. The Shield was once covered by huge slabs of ice that were more than 2 miles (3.2 kilometers) thick in places. This heavy ice sheet moved outward in all directions, scouring and gouging the bedrock beneath it and carving out the NWT's valleys, lakes, basins, and deep coastal fjords. When the glaciers that covered the lowlands of the NWT melted at the end of the most recent Ice Age, about 10,000 years ago, their waters became rivers and lakes. Today more than 51,000 square miles (132,090 square kilometers) of the NWT is covered by fresh water, making up 9.2 percent of the world's freshwater reserves.

Along the seacoast, the flat terrain of the tundra is broken in places by pingos, dome-shaped hills with cores of ice.

Some parts of the Canadian Arctic are still covered by glaciers, or large masses of land ice, that built up during the most recent Ice Age in the mountains and highlands of the Arctic islands and along the Yukon border. The Ice Age also deep-froze the rocky soil, creating permafrost. Permafrost is soil that remains at or below a temperature of 32 degrees Fahrenheit (0 degrees Celsius) for at least 2 years; most of the permafrost in the Northwest Territories has been frozen for centuries. Permafrost is generally covered by an upper layer of soil, called the active layer, that undergoes seasonal freezing and thawing. The far northern islands of the NWT have active layers that are less than 4 inches (10 centimeters) thick, covering permafrost that extends to depths of as much as 1,500 feet (455 meters). The coldest ground temperatures in the world are found on Ellesmere Island, the northernmost island in the Territories. Even in the Mackenzie Delta on the mainland—which is warm compared with the Arctic islands—permafrost underlies much of the land.

Despite its frozen ground, the NWT is not barren. It has two types of vegetation: tundra and taiga. North of the tree line, where the thin soil and cold climate prevent the growth of full-

The South Nahanni River slices through the Mackenzie Mountains and the boreal forests of the western Territories. Much of the river's course lies within Nahanni National Park, a magnificent region of gorges and waterfalls that has been named a World Heritage Site by the United Nations.

Ellesmere Island is the northernmost island in the Canadian Arctic. Bitterly cold in winter, with a landscape both forbidding and majestic, it is home to several Native communities as well as to military and meteorological stations.

size trees, is the tundra, a land of mosses and lichens, tough grasses, small shrubs, stunted or dwarf trees, and in the summer, a remarkable variety of wildflowers. South of the tree line is the taiga, a type of northern or boreal forest dominated by spruce, fir, and pine trees.

Three Regions

Geographers divide the Northwest Territories into three geographic regions: the Mackenzie Valley in the west, the Arctic Mainland in the east, and the Arctic Archipelago in the north.

The tree line runs from the southeast to the northwest through the Mackenzie Valley region. Only the northernmost part of this region is tundra; most of it is taiga. In the west, along the Yukon border, are the rugged Mackenzie Mountains, a northern continuation of the Rocky Mountains. They contain the highest peak in the NWT—Mt. Sir James MacBrien, with a height of 9,062 feet (2,746 meters).

Just east of the mountains is the Mackenzie Valley. There is little fertile soil in the valley, and summer rain is scarce. Poor drainage on the flat terrain creates large swamps and bogs when the active layer of the soil thaws each summer. In addition to these swamps, the Mackenzie Valley region contains major waterways. The Mackenzie is Canada's longest river—1,071 miles

(1,724 kilometers) from its headwaters in Great Slave Lake to its mouth in the Beaufort Sea—and drains an area of 680,000 square miles (1.7 million square kilometers). Two lakes feed the river. Great Bear Lake, with an area of 12,120 square miles (31,400 square kilometers), is the world's eighth largest freshwater lake. Great Slave Lake is the sixth deepest lake in the world, with a maximum depth of 2,022 feet (616 meters).

The Mackenzie Valley has the warmest temperatures in the Canadian north. About 65 percent of the NWT's population live in this region, which also contains most of the Territories' timber and mineral resources.

A second region of the NWT, the Arctic Mainland, is northeast of the tree line, between the Mackenzie Valley and Hudson Bay. Also called the Barren Lands, the Arctic Mainland consists of rolling, rocky tundra dotted with lakes and rivers and covered with dwarf willow and alder trees that grow along the ground like vines or creeping shrubs.

This region is inhabited by approximately 10 percent of the Territories' population, mostly Native Americans. It also has abundant mineral resources, but Native land claims have prevented widespread exploitation of these resources. However, nickel and gold have been mined in several places, and some exploration for oil and gas has taken place.

The third region of the NWT, the Arctic Archipelago, consists of the maze of islands and channels north of the Canadian mainland as well as the islands in Hudson, James, and Ungava bays. The Arctic Archipelago has two types of landscape: tundra in the south and ice and snow in the north. In the summer the channels and waterways between the islands are often clogged with blue-white icebergs, and in the winter many of them are frozen over.

About 25 percent of the Territories' population live in the southern part of the Arctic Archipelago region, especially on Baffin, Victoria, and King William islands. The northern part of the region, which is almost completely uninhabited, consists of the Queen Elizabeth Islands, an island group north of Baffin, Victoria, and Banks islands. The largest island in the Queen

Elizabeth group is Ellesmere, which also has the region's highest mountain—Mt. Barbeau in the United States Range, with an altitude of 8,584 feet (2,616 meters).

Wildlife

Many species of mammals, birds, and fish inhabit the Northwest Territories. The largest mammals are the polar bear, caribou, musk-ox, and wood buffalo. The huge, white-furred polar bear lives along the Arctic coast. It feeds mainly on seals, and in the winter it waits by holes in the ice to catch them when they come up to breathe. Polar bears can swim great distances and often hunt on ice floes far from land.

Caribou belong to the deer family. There are three species in the NWT: Peary caribou live in the Arctic islands; Barren Ground caribou graze on the tundra north of the tree line in summer and migrate south to Saskatchewan and Manitoba in winter; and woodland caribou live in the Mackenzie Valley forests. Caribou eat grasses, mosses, ground lichens, mushrooms, and leaves. The meat and skins of these large deer have been a major source of food and clothing for the Native American peoples of the NWT for centuries.

Musk-oxen are shaggy, horned members of the cattle family; their range is now limited to the Canadian Arctic and Greenland. They too feed on the shrubs and grasses of the tundra, and they also are hunted by Native groups for food and skins. In the past, the caribou and musk-ox populations were severely depleted by overhunting and starvation. The establishment of wildlife sanctuaries and government restrictions on hunting has helped to replenish their numbers. Wood buffalo, also called bison, live in the enormous, forested Wood Buffalo National Park, which is shared by the NWT and the province of Alberta.

Other mammals in the NWT include the moose, grizzly bear, beaver, fox (notably the silver or white arctic fox), hare, and muskrat. The pelts of foxes and beavers provided the basis of the Territories' first industry, the fur trade; hunting and trapping still contribute to the economy today.

Whales, walruses, and seals thrive in the waters off the Arctic coast. The narwhal, a species of tusked whale, lives mainly in Baffin Bay and nearby Lancaster Sound; it numbers approximately 20,000. The beluga, a white whale closely related to the narwhal, also lives in the Arctic waters. International restrictions have limited the hunting of these and other whales to Native peoples whose traditional economies depend upon whaling.

More than 200 species of birds can be seen in the Northwest Territories. Seabirds such as guillemots, murres, jaegers, terns, and gulls nest in immense crowded colonies on cliffs along the coast. Sandhill cranes, swans, and snow geese both feed and breed in the broad river deltas and swampy plains. Other species include eagles, snowy owls, falcons, loons, and white pelicans. The NWT is a particularly good breeding ground for many bird species because during the summer, when the tundra is covered by countless shallow ponds and puddles, mosquitoes and black flies hatch there by the trillions. Thick clouds of these flying pests make life miserable for humans, but they provide a feast for nesting birds and their young.

Walruses live in small packs on coastal ice in the Arctic, feeding on shellfish that they dig from the sea bottom with their tusks. A full-grown walrus can reach a length of 10 feet (3 meters) or more; its only enemies are human hunters and polar bears.

The aurora borealis—also called the northern lights—are streamers or curtains of shimmering, multicolored light that sometimes appear in the northern skies. The phenomenon is caused by electromagnetic activity in the earth's atmosphere.

Climate and Weather

The Northwest Territories has only two seasons, summer and winter. In the south, summer lasts from June through September, and the rest of the year is winter. Farther north, 10 months of dark, cold winter is followed by 2 months of bright, mild summer. Although cold, the NWT is generally fairly dry, with little rain or snowfall. In an average year, Montreal and Ottawa receive far more snow than Yellowknife, the capital of the NWT. The Mackenzie Valley receives about 15 inches (38 centimeters) of precipitation each year, whereas Ellesmere Island receives only 2.5 inches (6.4 centimeters). The Territories' rivers, bays, and sea passages are blocked with ice much of the time; the shipping season lasts from June or July through mid-October.

North of the Arctic Circle, which runs through the Northwest Territories, a phenomenon occurs that is sometimes called the midnight sun. Summer days are extraordinarily long in high latitudes, and in midsummer the sun shines for nearly 24 hours. The nights are like long twilights, with the sun on the horizon. Even in the southern part of the NWT, each June day has 20 hours of daylight. But the long midsummer days are offset by the long midwinter nights. Yellowknife receives only about 6.5 hours of light each day in January, and farther north there is almost no sunlight for several months.

The Northwest Territories can experience extreme temperatures. The highest temperature ever recorded there was 103°F (39°C) at Fort Smith, on the Alberta border. The lowest temperature, −71°F (−58°C), was recorded in Shephard Bay, on the Arctic coast. Temperatures are generally warmest in the Mackenzie Valley and around Great Slave Lake, south of the tree line, where summer temperatures average about 60°F (15°C) and winter temperatures average −15°F (−23°C). The Arctic coast is colder, with summer temperatures averaging 42°F (6°C) and winter temperatures averaging −25°F (−32°C). In the far north, deep in the Arctic Archipelago, temperatures never rise much above 25°F (−4°C), even in July, and January temperatures average −40°F (−40°C).

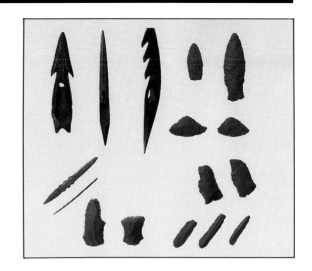

The History

The first Europeans to reach northern Canada arrived in A.D. 982, when a Viking explorer named Erik the Red sailed from the Viking colony in Greenland to the east coast of Baffin Island. For at least 200 years after his voyage, the Icelanders who colonized Greenland came to Arctic Canada to hunt in the summer.

The Vikings encountered Native Americans in Canada. Thousands of years before Erik's voyage, bands of nomadic tribespeople—descended from the peoples of Siberia and northwestern Asia—had migrated into the Canadian Arctic. Modern anthropologists refer to these early inhabitants as the Pre-Dorset people. The Pre-Dorset lived on the coast of the Northwest Territories from the Mackenzie Delta to the east coast of Baffin Island and as far north as Devon Island.

The Pre-Dorset hunted walruses, seals, and whales at sea as well as musk-oxen, caribou, and polar bears on land. Archaeological evidence suggests that the Pre-Dorset used lances and bows and arrows to kill their prey. They carved weapons and tools from stone, walrus ivory, and caribou antlers, and they lived in tents during the summer and snowhouses (later called igloos by the Europeans) during the winter.

An Inuit sculptor (opposite) carves a soapstone figure. The Inuit, who inhabited the Canadian Arctic when the first Europeans arrived, today number more than one-third of the Territories' population. They are the cultural heirs of the Pre-Dorset people, the earliest Native inhabitants of the Northwest Territories (NWT), who left scrapers, knives, arrowheads, and lance blades made of stone (above) on Baffin Island.

A family of Mackenzie Delta Inuit in the late 19th century. The Inuit lived in nomadic communities along the coast, in the Barren Lands, and in the Arctic Archipelago when the first Europeans arrived in the NWT.

Between 800 and 500 B.C., the Pre-Dorset were supplanted by a more sophisticated culture that archaeologists call the Dorset. The Dorset people inherited many of the characteristics of their ancestors, the Pre-Dorset, but they appear to have done more hunting on the sea ice than on land. They used kayaks to travel by water and hand-drawn sleds to journey across the frozen tundra. The Dorset left behind stone, ivory, and antler carvings of animals and people that have given archaeologists invaluable clues about how they lived.

The fate of the Dorset is one of the great mysteries of Arctic archaeology. No one is certain about what caused the decline of their culture, which seems to have disappeared around A.D. 1200, the era during which a new people called the Thule were arriving in the Canadian Arctic.

The Thule and the Inuit

The Thule were the ancestors of today's Inuit people. They came from the western Arctic, probably from Alaska, where they lived by hunting bowhead whales in the Beaufort Sea, and they were well equipped with the skills and tools required for life in the far north. They traveled in large open boats called umiaks and smaller, skin-covered kayaks. On land they used dogsleds. They fashioned bows and arrows, harpoons, and tools out of stone, bone, ivory, copper, and the skins and sinews of animals. The Inuit people who today inhabit the northern reaches of the vast region stretching from Quebec to Alaska are believed to be descended from the Thule; this is why all Inuit speak a common language (although with several different dialects) called Inuktitut or Inuttituut.

Starting around 1600, the Inuit culture began growing from Thule roots. The Inuit developed into six distinct but closely related groups in the Northwest Territories. From west to east along the coast there were the Mackenzie Delta, Copper, Netsilik, Igulik, and Baffinland Inuit. The only inland group, the Caribou Inuit, lived near present-day Baker Lake and derived their food, clothing, and shelter from the caribou rather than from the whales, seals, fish, and walruses favored by the coastal peoples. The six groups still live in their traditional territories today.

Apart from minor differences in dialect and tradition, these groups shared most cultural characteristics. All were nomadic hunters and gatherers, moving from one camp to another on a seasonal basis. They lived in bands of about five households each. A household consisted of a married couple and their children as well as elderly or unmarried relatives. Inuit life was communal: Hunting and most social activities depended upon the cooperation of everyone in the band, so a close sense of kinship and a readiness to share became—and remain—characteristic of Inuit culture.

The Thule, and later the Inuit, lived north of the tree line, but a different culture existed in the south—that of the Athapaskan-speaking peoples, who lived in the boreal forest of the Mackenzie River lowlands. These were the ancestors of today's Dene people.

The Dene

The immense sweep of forest and tundra between Hudson Bay and Alaska is, archaeologically speaking, one of the least-explored regions in Canada. There is evidence that Native Americans occupied this area at least 7,000 years ago.

Over time, seven distinct but related cultures developed among the inhabitants of the NWT's forest zone. Their languages were closely related and they shared many traditions. Collectively they became known as the Dene (pronounced DEH-nay). The largest group was the Chipewyan tribes. They were also the southernmost Athapaskan people, inhabiting the area south of Great Slave Lake. The Chipewyan were the first to accompany European explorers and fur traders into the northern part of the NWT. A people called the Slave or Slavey also lived near Great Slave Lake, and the Dogrib people lived north of them. The Yellowknife lived northeast of Great Slave Lake, on the border of the Barren Lands. To the northwest, in the valley of the Mackenzie River, lived a small group called the Hare. The Nahanni lived in the southern part of the Mackenzie Mountains. The Kutchin, the northernmost Native people in North America other than the Inuit, lived near the present-day border with the Yukon Territory.

All these Dene groups lived by gathering wild plants, hunting, fishing, and trapping. They were nomadic, following the migrations of the game they hunted. Their hunting implements included bows, several types of arrows, and a variety of traps and snares. Fish were caught with nets, traps, spears, and hooks and lines. The Dene also gathered berries, which they dried and preserved in the fall to eat during the winter or pounded into dried meat and grease to make the food called pemmican. In the winter they traveled by snowshoe, toboggan, and sled; in the summer they used canoes on the rivers and the lakes.

Although the Inuit and the Dene lived in separate parts of what is now the NWT, the two peoples probably encountered one another in the Barren Lands when the Inuit followed the caribou south and the Dene followed the herds north. Apparently they made war on each other, for by the time Europeans arrived in the region, the Inuit and the Dene were enemies. It is believed that the Dene coined the term *Eskimos*, which was used for many years to refer to the Inuit. It means "eaters of raw flesh" in one

English navigator Martin Frobisher explored the coast of Baffin Island in the late 16th century. He loaded several ships with rocks from the island, thinking he had found gold, but his cargo was later determined to be worthless.

In 1610, Henry Hudson's mutinous crew set the explorer adrift in a small boat in the bay that today bears his name. The mutineers returned to England, but Hudson and his loyal followers were never seen again.

of the Athapaskan dialects and probably referred to the Inuit practice of eating raw seal and whale meat. The Dene meant the name as an insult, and it is no longer used. The Inuit had an equally low opinion of the Dene: Some Inuit believed that the Dene (and later, the Europeans) had been created by the mating of an Inuit woman and a dog.

Exploration and Exploitation

The seasonal fishing trips of the Norse Greenlanders in the waters around Baffin Island ended in the 13th century, when the Greenland colony died out, but a new wave of Europeans began to arrive in the 16th century. An Englishman named Martin Frobisher was probably the first European of this period to see the Northwest Territories. He arrived in 1576, searching for the Northwest Passage, a hoped-for sea route through North America; explorers searched for this fabled passage from the Atlantic Ocean to the Pacific Ocean because it would be the

For several centuries, the search for the elusive Northwest Passage drew ships and seamen into the hazardous maze of islands and channels north of the Canadian mainland. The pace of exploration increased during the search for Sir John Franklin's lost expedition.

shortest route from Europe to Japan, China, and other Asian lands. Frobisher made landfall on the east coast of Baffin Island and then sailed for 150 miles (256 kilometers) into the bay that now bears his name, before turning back.

Because he did not reach the end of Frobisher Bay, the navigator mistakenly believed he had found the Northwest Passage. Frobisher also mistakenly thought he had discovered gold on Baffin Island; he took home a handful of rocks that glittered with sparkling flecks and used them to win the support of Queen Elizabeth I, who sponsored two later journeys to the island to gather the gold-bearing ore. Unfortunately for the queen and other investors, Frobisher's rocks turned out to contain only iron pyrites, sometimes called fool's gold.

John Davis, another Englishman, made three summer voyages to North America in 1585, 1586, and 1587. He discovered Davis Strait, which leads into Baffin Bay, and he explored Cumberland Sound on the east coast of Baffin Island.

Both Frobisher and Davis knew that there was a great gulf between Baffin Island and the northernmost point of Labrador (now part of Quebec), but neither had been able to explore it. In 1610, Henry Hudson, another English navigator who hoped to find the Northwest Passage, sailed into that gulf through what is now called the Hudson Strait. He followed the strait into another vast body of water, which he hoped was the Northwest Passage, but he was unable to complete his investigation. His mutinous crew set Hudson, Hudson's son, and a few loyal sailors adrift in a small boat, and they were never seen or heard from again. Later explorers proved that Hudson had entered a large bay, which was named after him.

In the decades that followed, many other European explorers ventured into the Canadian Arctic. Among them were Thomas Button, Jens Munck, Luke Foxe, and Thomas James. These intrepid travelers did not discover the Northwest Passage, but they mapped the eastern Arctic, especially the west coast of Hudson Bay. By the middle of the 17th century, exploring the Canadian interior and garnering its resources had become as important to both the British and the French as finding the Northwest Passage.

In 1670, the British government gave exclusive trading rights in an enormous tract of Canada to the Hudson's Bay Company (HBC), a British fur-trading concern. The HBC's territory included what is now northern Quebec and Ontario, all of Manitoba, most of Saskatchewan, southern Alberta, and the east coast of the Northwest Territories. This region was named Prince Rupert's Land, and the HBC established a flourishing fur trade within its borders and beyond them.

In the southern part of Prince Rupert's Land, the company established fur-trading posts along the rivers as far west as Alberta. In the north, however, merchants built posts only on the shores of Hudson Bay, inviting the Natives to bring them pelts from the interior. Occasionally the company sent an employee northwest to explore what lay beyond the perimeters of its territory. One of the most remarkable such journeys was made by Samuel Hearne from 1770 to 1772. With the aid of a Chipewyan guide named Matonabbee, he crossed the Barren Lands to Great Slave Lake and then made his way up the Coppermine River to the Arctic Ocean.

When Hearne returned to the HBC post at Churchill, Manitoba, after his 2,000-mile (3,200-kilometer) journey, he knew more about what is now the Northwest Territories than any other European. He had learned that the Barren Lands were indeed barren of most fur-bearing animals, except caribou and the ferocious polar bear, and that the Coppermine River was so shallow and difficult to traverse that it would be useless as a trade route. He also discovered that the Chipewyan and the Inuit were bitter enemies when he saw his guides massacre a troop of Inuit. Because of Hearne's discouraging report, it was many years before the HBC set up permanent posts in the north.

In the meantime, a rival trading firm called the North West Company (NWC) began moving into the Canadian interior. The Nor'westers, as its members were called, also numbered explorers in their ranks. The best known of them was Alexander Mackenzie, who in 1789 set out from Fort Chipewyan on Lake

The fate of the Franklin expedition captured the imagination of people around the world and was the subject of many tragic poems, paintings, and engravings. The bodies of some of Franklin's men have been found in the NWT, where they were buried by their comrades.

Athabasca in present-day Alberta. He canoed north on the Slave River to Great Slave Lake and then northwest along a large river that flowed out of the lake. Mackenzie followed this river for weeks, only to find that it emptied into the ice-fringed Beaufort Sea, not into the Pacific as he had hoped. The explorer was so downcast that he named the longest river in Canada the River of Disappointment. Today it is called the Mackenzie River.

Mackenzie's journey may have ended in disappointment for the explorer, but it created new trade opportunities for the NWC. Mackenzie reported that the forests along his river were teeming with fur-bearing animals, and the Nor'westers immediately set up trading posts to collect pelts. The HBC, too, wanted to trade in the Mackenzie Valley, and rivalry between the companies intensified until 1821, when the HBC absorbed the NWC. The center of trading activity in the region was Great Slave Lake, which also served as the starting point for 19th-century expeditions along the Arctic coast.

The best-known 19th-century Arctic explorer was John Franklin, a captain in the British Royal Navy who was asked by the British government to chart the unknown Arctic seaboard of North America. Britain wanted both to increase geographic knowledge and to set a limit to Russian expansion eastward from Alaska (Russia did not sell Alaska to the United States until 1867).

Franklin made three trips into the Arctic. The first, from 1819 to 1822, was an overland expedition that surveyed the region from Hudson Bay to Great Slave Lake, north along the Coppermine River, and along the ice-choked Arctic shoreline. The expedition was successful until Franklin, fearing that he and his party would not find a river route back to the lake, attempted an overland route through unknown territory. He lost 10 men to starvation and cold.

Undaunted, Franklin embarked on a second trek in 1825. He took a small fleet north up the Mackenzie River and then went west, surveying the icy, fogbound seacoast as far west as Prudhoe Bay, Alaska, where bad weather forced him to turn back. He arrived back at camp in 1827.

Norwegian explorer Roald Amundsen was the first to complete the Northwest Passage by sea, from 1903 to 1906. In 1911, Amundsen became the first to reach the South Pole. He died in the Arctic in 1928; his plane disappeared while he was searching for a fellow explorer who was lost.

Nearly 20 years passed before Franklin's third and final expedition. In the meantime, explorers such as George Back, William Edward Parry, Thomas Simpson, and John Rae charted much of the Arctic Archipelago. In 1829, John Ross experimented with steam propulsion in the Arctic; he brought a paddle wheeler into Prince Regent Inlet, between Baffin Island and the Boothia Peninsula, but was stranded when the ship was surrounded by fast-forming ice. Ross and his men were forced to abandon the ship. They lived on the Boothia Peninsula for three years, helped by friendly Inuit, before making their way back to European settlements.

Despite the dangers, the search for the Northwest Passage continued. Franklin—now Sir John Franklin, for he had been knighted in 1828—left on his final voyage in 1845 with 128 men. His ships, the *Erebus* and the *Terror*, sailed from England on May 19. They were last sighted in late July, headed for Lancaster Sound, and Franklin and his men were never seen alive again by Europeans. Many search parties set out to look for them, spurred on by the British government and the grieving Lady Franklin, but it was 14 years before the fate of the expedition was known. Relics, including corpses and written records, were located, revealing that in 1846 the ships had been frozen in by pack ice in the Victoria Strait, one of the many ice-choked channels in the northern maze. The crews waited for the ships to break free, but they never did. Franklin died in 1847, and by then many others were dead as well. In April 1848 the survivors abandoned the ice-locked vessels, hoping to make their way over ice and land to some outpost of civilization. They died in the wilderness, leaving relics that were found by later travelers in the Arctic.

As a result of the wide-ranging search for the Franklin expedition, the map of the Canadian Arctic was finally completed, and the long-sought-after Northwest Passage was found. The first to travel through the passage was Robert McClure, a British commander who made the passage in 1854, although he was unable to sail all the way because of heavy pack ice and had to complete the journey on foot. The first to navigate the Northwest Passage entirely by ship was the Norwegian polar explorer Roald Amundsen, who made the trip from 1903 to 1906. These men proved that a Northwest Passage through North America does exist, although it is too cold and difficult for commercial shipping.

Meanwhile, the whaling industry flourished in the Arctic Archipelago during the 19th century. For centuries the Inuit had hunted many species of whales in the frigid Arctic waters. During the 17th century, they were joined by European whalers, who hunted on the eastern side of the Davis Strait near Greenland. Soon American and European whaling camps existed on Baffin Island and elsewhere in the Arctic Regions.

The whale was central to Inuit life. The Inuit ate the whale's skin, blubber, flesh, and internal organs. They built homes, furniture, and tools out of whalebones, and they burned whale oil for heat and light.

The Europeans extracted oil from the blubber for streetlamp fuel and for making soap, margarine, paints, and varnishes. Another desirable substance was baleen, which is a tough, flexible material that hangs in long strips from the roof of the bowhead whale's mouth. In the 19th and early 20th centuries, it was used to make buggy whips, corset stays, and fishing rods. Europeans and Americans whaled in the Arctic waters for nearly a century. Whaling activity peaked from 1820 to 1840; during these 2 decades, the yearly catch often exceeded 1,000 whales. The effect on the Arctic environment and on the lives of the Inuit was dramatic. Caribou herds were decimated to feed the whalers, and as animal supplies dwindled, the Natives began to rely on food and clothing provided by the Europeans. Natives were employed as pilots, hunters, and dog drivers; the introduction of wage-paying jobs changed their traditional economy. Furthermore, the Europeans brought diseases against which the American Natives had never developed immunities. Entire communities of both Inuit and Dene were wiped out by epidemics of measles, typhus, and scarlet fever.

Until about 1915, whaling in the Canadian Arctic continued unchecked. By that time the whales had been driven to near extinction. But the demand for baleen had decreased consider-

Miners at Port Radium in 1946. The mining of radioactive ores began around Great Bear Lake in the 1930s.

ably, and as early as the 1930s, laws were enacted to protect the bowhead whale. Since then restrictions have expanded to include all species of whales, and they are honored by most nations of the world. The Inuit, however, are allowed to engage in traditional whale hunts at certain times and places.

The 20th Century

From the earliest days of exploration, the land that is now the Northwest Territories had been controlled by the British government and the Hudson's Bay Company. Then, in 1867, the British colonies in southeastern Canada declared their independence from Great Britain and joined together to form a new country called the Dominion of Canada. In 1870, the new Canadian government bought Prince Rupert's Land from the Hudson's Bay Company. From Great Britain, Canada also acquired territory north and west of Prince Rupert's Land, as well.

These new land acquisitions were divided into provinces and territories. Manitoba was created in 1870, the Yukon Territory in 1898, and Alberta and Saskatchewan in 1905. The most recent adjustment of the NWT's borders occurred in 1912, when the Territories' Ungava Peninsula on the southeastern side of Hudson Bay was given to Quebec; Manitoba and Ontario, too, acquired some land tracts from the NWT at that time.

For decades, the Northwest Territories was largely ignored by the rest of North America. Its remoteness and harsh climate discouraged settlement and development. Some Europeans came into the region to serve at Royal Canadian Mounted Police posts or other federal agencies in the Mackenzie Valley, but there were few homesteaders. In the early years of the 20th century, the Territories' mineral resources generated a surge of interest and immigration, and World War II (1939–45) accelerated development as well.

During the war, the NWT's strategic location and large mineral reserves became important to both Canada and the United States. Airstrips and military posts were quickly built, especially along the Arctic coast, to protect North America from enemy attack; weather stations were based in the Arctic to help forecast conditions in the North Atlantic war zone; and a 400-mile (640-kilometer) oil pipeline was built to carry oil from the NWT across the Mackenzie Mountains to Whitehorse in the Yukon Territory.

In the following decades, during the cold war of the 1950s and 1960s, when hostility between the Soviet Union and the United States was at its height, the NWT was considered a strategic outpost situated between the two superpowers. If a Soviet attack were launched across the North Pole toward the United States, it would have to cross the Canadian Arctic, and U.S. military experts wanted to build warning stations in the Arctic to alert them of such an attack in time to protect major U.S. cities. Therefore, in November 1954, Canada and the United States agreed to build the Distant Early Warning System (usually called the DEW line) along the Arctic coast from Alaska to Baffin Island. A string of 22 radar stations was constructed, largely by workers from the Northwest Territories.

Since the 1970s, the DEW line has lost much of its importance, partly because of an easing of cold war tensions but also because contemporary weaponry, such as the cruise missile, has made its technology obsolete. In 1985, Canada and the United States agreed to create a new radar line. Called the North Warning System, it is being developed along the Arctic coast.

One of the foremost issues in the Northwest Territories during the 1980s was the question of political status. The NWT and its neighbor, the Yukon Territory, have a different status within Canada than the country's 10 provinces; their land-use policies, natural resources, taxes, administration, and Native affairs are largely controlled by the federal government, and there is less autonomy than in the provinces.

But the people of the Northwest Territories have been seeking provincial status. They believe that if the NWT becomes a province, they will gain more control over natural resources

A radar station along the DEW line (from Distant Early Warning System), which was built across the Arctic in the 1950s to warn of an attack from the Soviet Union across the North Pole.

and economic development and reap greater benefits from such development. The federal government generally supports this goal and has gradually increased the powers of the two territories' local administrations.

The issue of provincial status cannot be resolved, however, until it is determined whether to turn the NWT into one province or two. The Inuit, who constitute about 85 percent of the population north and east of the tree line, want their lands to become a separate Inuit territory or province, to be called Nunavut ("our land"). Most Dene and Europeans, who are concentrated in the Mackenzie Valley region, are opposed to the Inuit proposal.

In April 1982, the people of the NWT voted in a special referendum on the issue of dividing the territory. Fifty-six percent of voters favored the division. More than 90 percent of the Inuit voted for the division, whereas the predominantly European communities in Yellowknife, Hay River, and Inuvik voted against it. The Dene have announced that if a division does occur, they want to establish their own separate political entity, to be called Denendeh.

In November 1982, the federal government endorsed a plan to divide the Territories into two independent jurisdictions. Nearly 10 years later, the division had not yet taken place because the nature and borders of the new territories are still in dispute. It is likely that the issues of land division and provincial status will dominate the political life of the NWT well into the 1990s.

Dennis Patterson, the government leader of the Northwest Territories in 1991, ice fishes in traditional Inuit garb. The government leader is a member of the legislative assembly and serves as the NWT's highest executive official.

The Economy

Although the earliest economic activities in the Northwest Territories focused upon natural resources such as wildlife and mineral ore, today more people in the NWT work in the public service sector than in any other business or industry. The government is the Territories' largest employer; one-fifth of the labor force works for the federal, territorial, or municipal administrations, which include health care and education facilities. Nevertheless, the resource-based industries continue to play an important part in the Territories' economy.

Mining

When Alexander Mackenzie was journeying along the river that now bears his name, he noticed a liquid that resembled yellow wax seeping from the ground in what is now Norman Wells. In the early 20th century, the gooey liquid was found to be oil. The Territories' first oil wells were dug in 1919, but it was not until World War II that this resource was fully appreciated. To supply

Opposite: The grave of a whaler near Pond Inlet, Baffin Island, marks the site of a 19th-century whaling colony. Once a leading industry in the region, commercial whaling has been outlawed by an international ban, although Native hunters are permitted to harvest whales in limited quantities.
Above: A craftsman displays a figure carved from soapstone. Native arts and crafts, exported for sale to collectors all over the world, have considerable economic as well as cultural importance in the Northwest Territories.

fuel for the defense of Alaska, the United States government constructed the Canol pipeline to carry oil through the Mackenzie Mountains to the Yukon city of Whitehorse, and the Norman Wells oil field expanded from 4 to 64 wells. When the war was over, however, the pipeline was abandoned.

Today oil flows south from the NWT instead of west. The Norman Wells–Zama pipeline, completed in 1985, brings an average of 3,000 barrels of oil every day to the province of Alberta. When production is at its peak, the Norman Wells oil field can produce 25,000 barrels a day.

The Northwest Territories has abundant mineral resources in addition to oil and gas. In the 1890s, prospectors on their way to the Klondike gold rush in the Yukon discovered some gold near Yellowknife. Radium was discovered at the eastern end of Great Bear Lake in 1930. Mines were opened in the area, and a few years later, when the world entered the nuclear age, the Territories' reserves of radioactive ores became increasingly important. Zinc, lead, nickel, copper, silver, and tungsten have

A pipeline carries oil from wells on an island in the Mackenzie River near Norman Wells, where oil was spotted by explorer Alexander Mackenzie in the 18th century.

Arctic char dry in the sun in Wager Bay, near the Arctic Circle. Char belong to the salmon family and are the principal catch in the northern waters.

also been mined. The tiny settlement of Tungsten in the western NWT marks the site of the Territories' largest tungsten mine; although it was closed in the 1980s because of falling prices for this mineral, it once provided 100 percent of Canada's tungsten. Close to 2,000 people are employed by the mining industry in the NWT.

Hunting and Trapping

Most families in the smaller communities of the NWT supplement their incomes by hunting, trapping, and fishing. Officially, however, only about 5,000 residents hold commercial hunting and trapping licenses. The Territories account for about 10 percent of Canada's production of wild fur. Animals trapped include foxes, lynx, marten, and seals.

Before the 1980s, the Northwest Territories' fur trade earned $5 million to $7 million each year, but contemporary concerns for animal rights and conservation have reduced the market for wild fur. The Inuit sealskin trade has been particularly hard hit. For much of the 20th century, the Inuit could count on selling more than 20,000 sealskins each year—sometimes for as much as $65 each—to fur manufacturers, who used the skins to make luxury coats. After environmental organizations publicized the brutal clubbing of baby seals during the 1970s and 1980s,

Campers and supplies are transported by seaplane to sites on the Territories' many rivers and lakes. The appeal of rugged outdoor adventure draws thousands of visitors each year, making tourism an increasingly significant segment of the territorial economy.

however, the market for sealskin all but disappeared. Ironically, the hunters condemned by environmentalists were international commercial sealers, not the Inuit, who use guns and kill only adult seals. In the early 1990s, South Korea and Japan began importing sealskins—not for coats but for leather goods, such as wallets, gloves, and automobile seats.

Fishing and Farming

Commercial fishing in the NWT brings in revenues of about $1.75 million each year. Almost all commercial fishing takes place on Great Slave Lake, where whitefish and lake trout are the most important catches. In the north, the main catch is arctic char, a member of the salmon family that spawns in fresh water.

Agriculture plays a minor role in the NWT's economy. Although the warm summers, with their long hours of sunlight, encourage some farming, the frequent summer droughts and the limited amount of good soil have made it nearly impossible for farmers to make a profit. It is far less expensive for residents of the Territories to import fruits and vegetables from the southern provinces than to grow them.

Manufacturing and Handicrafts

The Northwest Territories does not have a large manufacturing sector. Petroleum products, wood products, and printed materials are some of the items made in the few factories, located mostly in the capital of Yellowknife or in the more northern city of Inuvik.

The sale of Native art and handicrafts, however, is increasingly important to the economy. Since the 1960s, the Natives of the Territories have embarked on a vigorous program to develop the trade of their arts and crafts, which now earns several million dollars each year. More than one-sixth of the Native population contribute to the arts, creating soapstone sculptures, embroidered clothing, paintings, and prints.

Most Inuit works are sold by one of about 50 Native cooperatives. The cooperatives were established by the federal government in the 1950s to introduce the Inuit to a cash economy. At first, the co-ops produced goods for local consumption only. They have since expanded their operations, marketing local products worldwide, importing goods from the south, and introducing a variety of new services, including hotels, restaurants, and retail stores. The co-ops are the largest employers of Natives in the Territories. One of the best-known co-ops is the West Baffin Co-op at Cape Dorset, which produces and markets Inuit prints and carvings.

Many people in the Territories hope that tourism will stimulate their economy. The spectacular scenery and unique cultural heritage of the Canadian Arctic draw about 90,000 visitors to the Territories every year; in 1989, tourists spent about $88 million in the NWT. The role of tourism in the territorial economy is certain to increase, and the people of the NWT hope to benefit from it without allowing the tourist trade to damage their land or their way of life.

The People

The population of the Northwest Territories is just over 52,000. About 42 percent of the population are of European descent, 35 percent are Inuit, and 17 percent are Dene. Another 6 percent of the people are Métis, persons of mixed Native and European ancestry.

Most of the Inuit live in the interior of the Arctic Mainland, around the shores of Hudson Bay, and on Baffin Island and the other islands of the Arctic Archipelago. They hunt and trap, sell arts and crafts, work for the government, or act as tourist guides. The Europeans live mostly in the Mackenzie Valley area. They are employed mainly by the government, the mining industry, and the small businesses located in the capital of Yellowknife and other larger communities. The Dene too inhabit the Mackenzie Valley region. Some of them still live off the land as they have for centuries; others work for government agencies, in industry and commerce, and in tourism. Even those Dene who work in industry often supplement their income by hunting and trapping.

Opposite: An Inuit woman scrapes a caribou hide, from which she will later make clothing. Although modern technology in the form of the rifle, the television, and the snowmobile has changed the lives of many Inuit, traditional practices are still part of everyday life.
Above: Boys in Rankin Inlet cycle past a satellite dish—one of the many such installations that have put even the most remote communities in the Territories in touch with the rest of the world.

The Métis, once considered by the government to be part of the Dene nation, are now claiming a separate identity as a fourth ethnic group in the Territories. They too live primarily in the Mackenzie Valley region.

Life for the Natives of the Northwest Territories has changed dramatically since the first Europeans explored the Arctic landscape. The snowmobile has largely replaced the dogsled in Inuit communities, and the gun has replaced the bow and arrow. All but the most remote communities are connected to the modern world through television. Satellite channels now make it possible to transmit radio and TV programs to all territorial communities with populations over 150, and the satellite dish has become a familiar component of the landscape. An Inuit family in the isolated village of Spence Bay, thousands of miles from the nearest city, can tune into the nightly news or prime-time entertainment as easily as can a family in Toronto or New York. Radio broadcasts are made in 10 Native languages and dialects as well as in English and French.

Although the modern world has had a significant impact on the lives of the Natives, they have made great efforts to protect and cultivate their traditional cultures. Schools and government programs recognize and encourage Native arts, languages, and traditions.

Education

Until World War II, education in the Territories was provided chiefly by church missions, and schools were few and far between. But starting in 1959, a federal program developed a territorial school system that embraces nearly every major community. About 72 government-operated schools now employ about 800 teachers throughout the Territories. More than 13,000 students in grades 1 through 12 study in schools located close to home; high school students from particularly isolated areas often attend school in larger communities, living in local residences during the term.

An Inuit man prepares to coat the runners of his dogsled with heated mud. After the mud cools, he will smooth it with his knife, making a slippery surface that will glide across the snow.

A log schoolhouse in the town of Jean Marie River, west of Great Slave Lake. In the late 1950s, Canada's federal government undertook a program to build schools and introduce educational programs throughout the Territories; 72 schools now serve about 13,000 students.

In 1969, the federal government turned over the operation and administration of the school system to the territorial government. School districts are now financed by both local taxes and grants from the territorial government.

Arctic College, with branches in Fort Smith, Iqaluit, Inuvik, Rankin Inlet, and Cambridge Bay, is the Territories' only institution of higher learning. A two-year junior college and technical school, Arctic offers trade, professional, and occupational programs relating to the local economy. Also, the territorial government provides funds to help support students who wish to study in colleges and universities located outside the Territories.

The Arts

Cultural life in the Northwest Territories emphasizes Native arts, crafts, and traditions. Government-sponsored Native cultural and language programs have been established in several communities. The Prince of Wales Northern Heritage Centre in Yellowknife, with an extensive museum and archive, is the research center for the study of history and Native life in the Northwest Territories.

Inuit arts and handicrafts are treasured in the Territories and around the world. Since prehistoric times, the Inuit have decorated their garments with elaborate artwork and carved intricate animal and human forms from bones and ivory. When European fur traders and whalers first arrived in the Arctic, the Inuit traded these craft items for weapons, tools, and other European goods.

In the 1940s, a young artist from Toronto named James Houston came to the Arctic. He had studied painting and sculpture in France and had been hired by the Canadian government to work with Inuit artists; his job was to encourage the Inuit to produce, market, and sell their works, thus boosting the local economy. Since that time, the fine soapstone and ivory carvings and bright red-and-black prints made by Inuit artists have become known throughout the world. Traditionally, the content of Inuit art is based on the animals, birds, and marine life of the Arctic, although many artists use native myths and legends as their subject matter as well.

Both the Dene and the Inuit cultures have centuries-old myths and legends. But because they did not have written languages until fairly recently, their history and folklore have been passed down from generation to generation through the tradition of storytelling. To preserve this legacy, the government recently began a program to record the many stories and legends recounted by elderly Natives.

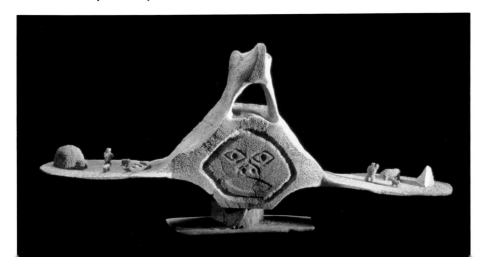

An Inuit bone carving. The panel on the left side of the central face bears the tiny figures of a man, a snowhouse, several sled dogs, and a sled; on the right are a man and a polar bear.

Recreation

Long before Europeans arrived in the Canadian Arctic, the Natives of the Northwest Territories competed in sports and games strikingly similar to those of European cultures. A form of volleyball, for example, was played with balls made of hide or sealskin and filled with caribou hair or grass. Today, sports in the Territories include both traditional Native games and popular modern sports such as soccer, hockey, and baseball.

A church in Inuvik, built in the form of a traditional snow-house, or igloo.

Wrestling is one of the athletic contests at the Arctic Winter Games, held every two years for competitors from the Northwest Territories, the Yukon, and Alaska. Inuit sports, practiced for centuries as tests of skill and endurance, are also featured at the games.

The Arctic Winter Games are designed to provide northern athletes with opportunities for training and competition. Held every two years since 1970, the games draw competitors from the Northwest Territories, the Yukon, and Alaska for events in badminton, hockey, indoor soccer, cross-country skiing, curling, and figure skating. The NWT regularly takes its turn hosting the games. A special feature of the Arctic Winter Games is the traditional sports developed over centuries by the Inuit. These sports test stamina, strength, and endurance in a variety of ways, as in the high kick, in which athletes leap as high into the air as they can with one foot or both feet. The Inuit also participate in archery, tug-of-war games, and wrestling.

The Inuit are also known for games that develop memory, patience, and manual dexterity. In the cup and pin game, for instance, the object is to toss up a cup (a carved piece of horn or bone with several holes drilled in it) and catch it on a pointed wooden stick. A story often accompanies the game; the holes in the cup represent incidents in the story and therefore must be speared in the proper order. Another game involves making figures out of string using only the rapid movements of one's fingers and thumbs.

The Communities

The Northwest Territories is sparsely populated. If the population of the NWT were distributed evenly across the land, there would be 25 square miles (65 square kilometers) per person. Nearly half the population, however, is concentrated in just 5 towns: Yellowknife, Inuvik, Hay River, Iqaluit, and Fort Smith have a combined population of about 24,000. Another 65 or so small communities, most containing fewer than 500 people, are scattered throughout the Territories. The government of the NWT divides the territory into six travel zones, each with its own population center.

The Baffin zone includes Baffin Island and other islands in the eastern Arctic. It is a rugged region of mountains and glaciers, home to musk-oxen, Peary caribou, foxes, wolves, and polar bears. Its landscape is one of snowy, ice-capped mountains, icy blue water, and—during the short summers—tundra plateaus and valleys filled with colorful Arctic flowers.

Approximately 23,000 people, most of them Inuit, live in 14 communities on the shores of fjords and inlets. The largest town, with about 3,000 residents, was formerly called Frobisher Bay; it

Opposite: Pond Inlet, on the northwest coast of Baffin Island, is built on the site of ancient habitations; archaeologists say that Inuit campsites and other relics near Pond Inlet are among the oldest in the Canadian Arctic. *Above:* The setting sun of a long northern twilight gleams on the skyline of Yellowknife, the Territories' capital and largest city.

has been renamed Iqaluit, which means "place of fish" in the Inuit language. A regional service and government center, Iqaluit has restaurants that serve Arctic char and musk-oxen as well as snowmobiles that compete with dogsleds for passengers. The town of Pangnirtung, on Cumberland Sound, is renowned as a center of Inuit arts and crafts. Another community, Grise Fiord, located on the south coast of Ellesmere Island, is the northernmost town in North America.

The Inuit of the Arctic coast zone were among the last Canadian Natives to be contacted by explorers and traders from the outside world. Today their ancient heritage is expressed in prints, sculptures, and tapestries that have brought them worldwide renown.

About 2,000 people live in 7 small communities along the Arctic coast. The largest is Cambridge Bay, also called Ikaluktutiak ("fair fishing place"), with more than 1,000 people. It is located on Victoria, the second largest island of the Arctic Archipelago. Cambridge Bay is the transportation and administration center of the region and has a cooperative fish plant that processes more than 110,000 pounds of arctic char every summer. The tiny town of Gjoa Haven on nearby King William Island is perched on the edge of what Norwegian explorer Roald Amundsen called "the finest little harbor in the world."

The town of Baker Lake, in the heart of the Barren Lands, is blanketed with snow during the winter months. It is the only inland community of Inuit in the Arctic and is set in the center of a vast expanse of tundra, home to herds of musk-oxen and caribou.

The people of Inuvik, like those of many northern communities around the world, add color to the landscape with vividly painted houses. Built in the 1950s in the delta of the Mackenzie River, Inuvik was a boomtown during the 1970s, when exploration for oil and natural gas took place in the nearby Beaufort Sea.

The Big River zone gets its name from the Mackenzie River, called the Dehco in Athapaskan. The first trading post in the Northwest Territories was built near present-day Fort Resolution in 1786. Located on the southeast shore of Great Slave Lake, Fort Resolution is now a rural community of about 500 European and Chipewyan residents.

Hay River is the largest community in the Big River region. With a population of about 3,000, it is the transportation hub of the north. Hay River is the southernmost port on the Mackenzie River system, servicing tugs and barges that go north to the Arctic Ocean. It also serves as headquarters of Great Slave Lake's commercial fishing industry, which supplies North America with whitefish.

The Keewatin zone stretches from the west coast of Hudson Bay inland to the heart of the Barren Lands. It is a region of austere beauty. Two major wildlife sanctuaries are located here: The Thelon Game Sanctuary, located in the center of the Barren Lands, was established in 1927 to protect the diminishing caribou herds, and the McConnell River Bird Sanctuary, near the town of Arviat, on Hudson Bay, is the nesting ground for some 400,000 snow geese.

About 5,000 people, mostly Inuit, live in the Keewatin's 7 major communities. Arviat is the artistic and cultural capital of the Keewatin and the site of the Inuit Cultural Institute, a museum and archive of eastern Arctic history and culture. Rankin Inlet, also on Hudson Bay, is the largest town in the Keewatin, with about 1,500 inhabitants. It is named after an explorer who visited the region in the 17th century, but it was not founded until 1955, when a nickel mine was opened there. Another Keewatin community, Repulse Bay, is located on the Arctic Circle.

The Northern Frontier zone lies between Great Slave and Great Bear lakes and has a population of more than 14,000 people in 8 major communities.

Yellowknife, the territorial capital, is the northernmost incorporated city in North America. Known as Sombak'e ("money place") in one of the Athapaskan dialects, Yellowknife is a bustling modern city of about 12,000 European and Native people. Located on the northern arm of Great Slave Lake, it serves as headquarters for the territorial government and other territory-wide organizations and agencies.

The capital is named for the Yellowknife band of Dene, who moved into the area in the late 18th century. The first European settlement was established after Alexander Mackenzie's 1789 expedition. Yellowknife remained a small trading post of fewer than 200 people until the gold rush of the 1930s turned it into the Territories' only boomtown. By 1940, more than 1,000 people had moved into the area. When a second gold rush occurred in the mid-1940s, the future of Yellowknife as a territorial center was assured. Gold mining continues near the city, primarily at the Giant Gold Mine, which was built at the end of World War II.

After the war, Yellowknife developed into a modern city. A hydroelectric dam built in 1948 alleviated the power shortages that often plagued the region and attracted residents and business and industry. In 1967, the federal government named Yellowknife the capital of the Territories and granted many administrative responsibilities to the territorial government.

Also, the Northern Frontier zone has the largest Dene settlement in the Northwest Territories. It is called Rae-Edzo and consists of two towns that were joined in the late 1960s. Fort

Rae, known in Dogrib as Behcho Ko ("big knife place"), was established as a Hudson's Bay Company post in 1904. Edzo, named after a Dogrib leader, was developed in the late 1960s by the federal government. About 1,400 Dogrib and Chipewyan people now live in the combined community.

The Western Arctic zone includes the broad valley of the Mackenzie River, the swampy lowlands of the Mackenzie Delta, the icy Beaufort Sea and Banks Island, and the high mountains of the Mackenzie range to the west. About 8,500 people live in about a dozen communities in the Western Arctic. Banks Island is the least settled area, although its wildlife attracts photographers and hunters. Its largest town is Sachs Harbour, with fewer than 200 inhabitants.

The newest and largest community is Inuvik ("place of man"), located near the mouth of the Mackenzie River. It was created by the federal government in 1954 to replace the town of Aklavik, which was thought to be sinking. Today both communities are starting points for camping and fishing expeditions in the Mackenzie Delta. Inuvik is also the administrative, communications, and fur-trading center of the lower Mackenzie River, with a population of approximately 3,400. Inuvik is notable for being the northernmost point reached by a North American public highway.

Arviat, on the shore of Hudson Bay, was founded as a trading post of the Hudson's Bay Company in the 1920s. Today it is a center for the study of the Inuit heritage; the Inuit Cultural Institute of Arviat has one of the world's largest collections of materials on the Arctic peoples. With a nearby bird sanctuary and a growing tourism business, Arviat represents three forces—cultural preservation, environmental protection, and economic development—that will shape the future of the Northwest Territories.

Things to Do and See

• **Kekerten Historic Park,** near Pangnirtung, Baffin Island: A late-19th-century whaling station. Stone building foundations and mounds show where Scottish and American whalers once lived, awaiting the arrival of bowhead whales in Cumberland Sound. Barrels, graves, old anchors, and the ribs of wrecked vessels are silent reminders of the "iron men in wooden ships" who came here looking for whales. Signs at the site help tell their story and that of the Inuit, who traded with the whalers for rifles, needles, and tobacco. Old photos give insight into the life and culture of both the Inuit and the whalers.

• **Qaummaarviit Historic Park,** on an island east of Iqaluit, Baffin Island: The park contains relics of cultures that have occupied this hunting ground over the past 2,600 years. The remains of several Thule winter dwellings have stone entranceways and walls ingeniously fitted together. More than 3,000 tools, dug from the tundra by archaeologists, are on display.

Opposite: An *inukshuk,* or Inuit trail marker, takes the form of a man striding across the Barren Lands.
Above: Moonrise on a summer night at Wager Bay.

Musk-oxen roam Arctic Canada in herds of 20 or 30 animals.

• **Northwest Passage Historic Park,** in Gjoa Haven, King William Island: Roald Amundsen, who first sailed the Northwest Passage, spent the winter before his journey with the Inuit at King William Island. The park commemorates European exploration over the centuries. A miniature replica of the *Gjoa* honors Amundsen; a display in the hamlet office features a large, colorful map that traces the routes of the Northwest Passage explorers; and a walking trail through the park leads to stone cairns that commemorate the daring feats of those early explorers. The role of the Native people in this era of northern exploration is documented with photos and artifacts.

• **Auyuittuq National Park Reserve,** Cumberland Peninsula, Baffin Island: Called the land that never melts, this park has majestic peaks, spectacular glaciers, and deeply etched river valleys. The Penny Ice Cap covers more than a quarter of the park's 8,300 square miles (21,500 square kilometers). Vegetation is sparse except during the brief Arctic summers, when wildflowers, such as the white mountain avens, yellow arctic poppy, and purple saxifrage, color the sand. Millions of seabirds nest on the coast, and polar bears, seals, walruses, and beluga whales swim in the icy coastal waters. From April to June, the park provides wilderness camping, hiking, and mountaineering.

• **Ellesmere Island National Park Reserve,** Ellesmere Island: Covering 15,250 square miles (39,500 square kilometers), this park is located in a region of perpetual ice and snow, with long winters and short, cool summers. Hundreds of glaciers extend into the valleys and fjords. Mt. Barbeau projects through the ice cover and towers over massive ice fields. Arctic hare, small herds of musk-oxen, caribou, arctic foxes, wolves, and a few polar bears inhabit the park, and at least 30 species of birds can be seen during the summer. Artifacts range from 4,000-year-old Inuit relics to the cairns and equipment left by European explorers of the late 19th and early 20th centuries.

• **Nahanni National Reserve,** Mackenzie Mountains: This United Nations World Heritage Site is located along the South Nahanni and Flat rivers near the western border of the NWT. It has deep canyons, rapids, waterfalls, hot springs, and rugged mountains. At Virginia Falls, the river takes a spectacular plunge of 300 feet (90 meters), more than twice the height of Niagara Falls.

• **Wood Buffalo National Park,** straddling the border between Alberta and the Northwest Territories: A United Nations World Heritage Site, this park is the second largest in the world. It is a subarctic wilderness of rivers, bogs, forests, lakes, and meadows. It has 4,500 bison, the largest free-roaming herd in the world, as well as the nesting grounds of the rare whooping cranes.

A bilingual stop sign in Baker Lake gives its message in English and Inuktitut.

Festivals

Sunrise Festival, early January, Inuvik: A celebration held each year on the night before the first day of sunlight, after more than a month of darkness.

Ookpik Carnival, mid-March, Hay River: A three-day carnival including an ice-carving contest, snowmobile races, hockey tournaments, log sawing, and dancing.

Caribou Carnival, end of March, Yellowknife: Ice hunting and tea brewing are just a few of the activities in this annual three-day festival. A parade opens the festivals, which include the Canadian Championship Dog Derby race, open to all dog mushers in North America.

Fun in the Snow Carnival, end of March, Norman Wells: Snowmobile races and curling tournaments in a western Arctic town.

Toonik Tyme, late April, Iqaluit: An annual festival celebrating the arrival of spring with traditional Inuit singing and dancing as well as contests in animal skinning, igloo building, and ice sculpting.

Pack ice covers the Arctic Sea near Alert, a base at the northern tip of Ellesmere Island.

Annual Midnight Sun Golf Tournament, June, Yellowknife: Golfers from all over Canada tee off at midnight on the first day of summer.

Midnight Sun Marathon, June, Nanisivik/Arctic Bay, north Baffin Island: One hundred runners from Canada and the United States compete in races between the communities of Nanisivik and Arctic Bay.

Folk on the Rocks, July, Yellowknife: An open-air event featuring Inuit and Dene performers as well as folk artists from the Arctic, southern Canada, and the United States.

NWT Fiddling Championship, August, Inuvik: An all-day event with barbecues and fiddling and jigging contests.

Dene Summer Games, August, Rae-Edzo: Boat races, Dene baseball, drum dances, tea brewing, and wood-chopping contests in the largest Dene community in the Territories.

Fall Fair, end of August, Yellowknife: The long hours of the northern summer result in a large harvest of vegetables in the Mackenzie Valley. Gardeners compete for prizes, and local artists and craftspeople display their work.

Arctic Christmas Festival, December, Spence Bay: A week of indoor games, drum dancing, and feasts on the Arctic coast.

Chronology

by 1000 B.C.	The Canadian Arctic is inhabited by the Pre-Dorset people and the Athapaskan-speaking people.
A.D. 982	Viking explorer Erik the Red visits Baffin Island.
by 1200	The Dorset have been replaced by the Thule and their descendants, the Inuit. The Dene peoples emerge from the Athapaskan language group.
1576	British explorer Martin Frobisher reaches Baffin Island in his search for the Northwest Passage.
1670	The British government gives Prince Rupert's Land to the Hudson's Bay Company (HBC).
1789	Alexander Mackenzie explores the Mackenzie River.
mid-19th century	The search for the Northwest Passage intensifies after Sir John Franklin's expedition is lost in the 1840s.
1870	Canada acquires Prince Rupert's Land from the HBC and soon acquires more territory in the north and west, forming the basis for today's Northwest Territories (NWT).
1930s and 1940s	A gold rush swells the population of Yellowknife; World War II spurs construction in the NWT.
1954	Canada and the United States agree to build the DEW line of radar stations across the Arctic.
1980s	The European, Inuit, and Dene inhabitants of the NWT move toward provincial status and the division of the NWT along ethnic lines.

Further Reading

Berton, Pierre. *The Arctic Grail: The Quest for the Northwest Passage and the North Pole.* New York: Viking Penguin, 1988.

Frideres, James. *Canada's Indians: Contemporary Conflicts.* Englewood Cliffs, NJ: Prentice-Hall, 1974.

Hocking, Anthony. *The Yukon and the Northwest Territories.* New York: McGraw-Hill Ryerson, 1979.

Holbrook, Sabra. *Canada's Kids.* New York: Atheneum, 1983.

Kurelek, William. *A Prairie Boy's Summer.* Boston: Houghton Mifflin, 1975.

Law, Kevin. *Canada.* New York: Chelsea House, 1990.

McNaught, Kenneth. *The Penguin History of Canada.* New York: Penguin Books, 1988.

Mead, Robert D. *Ultimate North: Canoeing Mackenzie's Great River.* Garden City, NY: Doubleday, 1976.

Newman, Peter C. *Caesars of the Wilderness: The Story of the Hudson's Bay Company.* New York: Penguin Books, 1988.

———. *The Company of Adventurers.* New York: Viking Penguin, 1985.

Perkins, Robert. *Into the Great Solitude: An Arctic Journey.* New York: Holt, Rinehart & Winston, 1991.

Ross, Eric. *Beyond the River and the Bay: The Canadian Northwest in 1811.* Toronto: University of Toronto Press, 1970.

Van Stone, James W. *Athapaskan Adaptations: Hunters and Fishermen of the Subarctic Forests.* New York: Harlan Davidson, 1974.

Watkins, Mel. *Dene Nation: The Colony Within.* Toronto: University of Toronto Press, 1977.

Woodcock, George. *The Canadians.* Cambridge: Harvard University Press, 1980.

Index

ACKNOWLEDGMENTS

The Bettmann Archive: pp. 20, 22, 26; Diana Blume: p. 6; Photo by Busse, courtesy of Northwest Territories Archives: p. 30; Richard Harrington, courtesy of Economic Development and Tourism, Northwest Territories: p. 56; Photo by Dan Heringa, courtesy of Economic Development and Tourism, Northwest Territories: pp. 3, 35, 54; Courtesy of Industry, Science and Technology, Canada: pp. 5, 11, 12, 18, 38, 41, 44, 46, 47, 48, 53, 59; Karpan photo: cover, pp. 8, 10, 36, 37, 40, 43, 50, 51, 55, 58; Photo by P & R Keough, courtesy of Economic Development and Tourism, Northwest Territories: p. 16; Photo by Jerry Kobalenko, courtesy of Economic Development and Tourism, Northwest Territories: p. 15; Library of Congress: pp. 23, 24, 27; National Museums of Canada: p. 19; Courtesy of Office of the Government Leader, Northwest Territories: p. 33; From the Permanent Collection of the "Prince of Wales Northern Heritage Centre, government of the Northwest Territories": p. 45; Photo by Gary Singer, courtesy of Economic Development and Tourism, Northwest Territories: p. 9; Debora Smith: p. 7; UPI/Bettmann Archive: p. 32; Photo by Douglas Walker, courtesy of Economic Development and Tourism, Northwest Territories: pp. 34, 49

Suzanne LeVert has contributed several volumes to Chelsea House's LET'S DISCOVER CANADA series. She is the author of four previous books for young readers. One of these, *The Sakharov File*, biography of noted Russian physicist Andrei Sakharov, was selected as a Notable Book by the National Council for the Social Studies. Her other books include *AIDS: In Search of a Killer, The Doubleday Book of Famous Americans*, and *New York*. Ms. LeVert also has extensive experience as an editor, first in children's books at Simon & Schuster, then as associate editor at *Trialogue*, the magazine of the Trilateral Commission, and as senior editor at Save the Children, the international relief and development organization. She lives in Cambridge, Massachusetts.

George Sheppard, General Editor, is a lecturer on Canadian and American history at McMaster University in Hamilton, Ontario. Dr. Sheppard holds an honors B.A. and an M.A. in history from Laurentian University and earned his Ph.D. in Canadian history at McMaster. He has taught Canadian history at Nipissing University in North Bay. His research specialty is the War of 1812, and he has published articles in *Histoire sociale/Social History, Papers of the Bibliographical Society of Canada*, and *Ontario History*. Dr. Sheppard is a native of Timmins, Ontario.

Pierre Berton, Senior Consulting Editor, is the author of 34 books, including *The Mysterious North, Klondike, Great Canadians, The Last Spike, The Great Railway Illustrated, Hollywood's Canada, My Country: The Remarkable Past, The Wild Frontier, The Invasion of Canada, Why We Act Like Canadians, The Klondike Quest*, and *The Arctic Grail*. He has won three Governor General's Awards for creative nonfiction, two National Newspaper Awards, and two ACTRA "Nellies" for broadcasting. He is a Companion of the Order of Canada, a member of the Canadian News Hall of Fame, and holds 12 honorary degrees. Raised in the Yukon, Mr. Berton began his newspaper career in Vancouver. He then became managing editor of *McLean's*, Canada's largest magazine, and subsequently worked for the Canadian Broadcasting Network and the *Toronto Star*. He lives in Kleinburg, Ontario.